DOGS IN TOWN
PAWTY TIME!

DOGS IN TOWN
PAWTY TIME!

FUN AND GAMES WITH OUR BEST FURRIENDS

echo
PUBLISHING

WELCOME

THIS IS MY HAPPY PLACE

DOGS
TOWN

ABOUT DOGS IN TOWN

Since 2016, Dogs in Town has supported over 10,000 dog parents in the Sydney area.

Why did we establish Dogs in Town? There are over 5 million dogs in Australia, and we noticed there were irregular standards of quality for the care of these furry individuals. We could see that dog parents were tired of searching for programs that would give their pooches quality exercise and the opportunity to socialise with other friendly pups. And we felt there was also a lack of services that focused on the different activity levels of individual dogs. Something needed to change. We believe that our dogs – your dogs – deserve the best. And so Dogs in Town was born.

We are a family-run, family-oriented business – a one-stop shop offering a full range of services for your fur babies. Basically we provide the support that *we* would want for *our* pups, to other furry families in Sydney.

Dogs in Town is experience-focused. We have a selective recruitment process in place to create a team of seasoned trainers, professional groomers, dog walkers and dog-loving experts. At each of our daycare centres – located in Alexandria, Marrickville and Paddington – we have a wealth of knowledge under one roof. In 2023, Dogs in Town was named the best dog-grooming service in Sydney for the second time in a row, from among 122 salons. Each of our centres features a creative and colourful, heathy and clean playground, which is combined with unparalleled supervision to offer a safe environment for pups.

Ultimately, Dogs in Town is a happy place for pooches, somewhere they can have 'real dog' life experiences, express themselves freely and be themselves!

Jakub Illes & Gustavo Montagut

www.dogsintown.com.au

dogsintownau

dogsintownalexandria

dogsintownmarrickville

dogsintownpaddington

WHAT'S HAPPENING IN THE HAPPIEST PLACE IN TOWN?

HAPPY
WELCOME
WELCOME
ABOUT DOGS

DOGS IN TOWN
ABOARD

All the dogs in town love ...

PLAYTIME IN THE PAWTY HOUSE

Playing and socialising are essential for your best furriend's health and happiness. It's time to run with the pack and raise the woof!

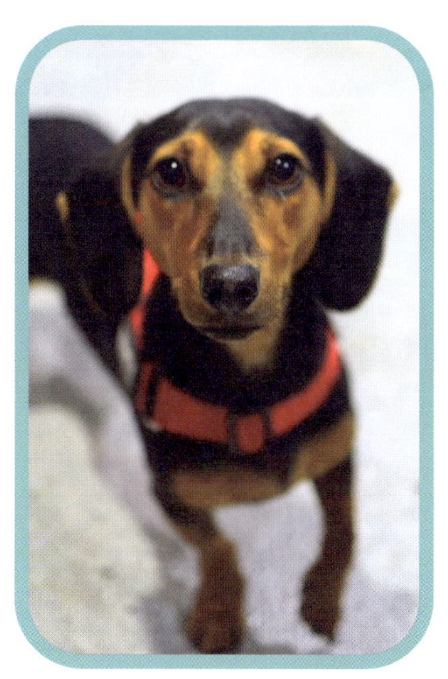

BE PAWS-ITIVE

Signs of a happy dog

Soft, 'floppy' ears.

Relaxed body language.

Mouth held slightly open.

A 'play bow', with their rear in the air and their chest lowered – i.e. an invitation to play!

A tail wag that makes their whole body wiggle.

Rolling onto their back to show their belly.

PUB
GEORGE
SULLEY

Having trouble getting your fur baby to exercise?

Walking your dog is the ideal way to keep them physically and mentally fit. Here are some more tips for other activities that will provide exercise and enrichment:

- Play games of fetch.
- Play tug of war.
- Play hide and seek (you hide and then call your pooch, and they have to find you).
- Hide your dog's dinner, so they have to hunt for it.
- Play scent games, and get your pup to sniff out treats and toys.
- Give them puzzle toys to play with.
- Use a 'snuffle mat' with raised strips of fabric to hide treats in.
- Make 'snuffle boxes' and DIY puzzles so they work for their meals.
- Set up an indoor obstacle course.
- Do plenty of training. It improves the level of your pup's obedience and gives them a mental and physical workout.

JUST BE
YOURSELF!

DOUBLE HAPPINESS

Tips for spending more time with your pup

- Schedule a DIY or professional spa day at least once a month.
- Commit to pet-friendly community activities.
- Spend time in the kitchen together.
- Take your pooch to work with you.
- Practise new tricks together.
- Take more selfies together.
- Run errands together.
- Read more books together.
- Cuddle more!

happy

PUPPIA

MY TIME TO SHINE

ICE CREAM

PUPPIA
PUPPIA

Teach your pooch how to sit down

Stand in front of your dog with a treat.

Hold the treat near their nose.

Lift the treat up and past their head. This naturally gets them to look up and sit down.

Reward your furry pal and repeat.

Have a barking good time

DOGGY
warehouse
FOOD
fit life
happy
puppies

TIME OUT!

How many hours a day do dogs sleep?

Pooches need much more sleep than we do, but the total hours of sleep each dog needs relies on a variety of factors. Age is the most important and has the greatest impact on a dog's sleep schedule.

Puppies: Indications are that most puppies need 11 hours' sleep a day.

Adults: Most adult dogs seem to need between 8 and 13.5 hours of shut-eye a day.

Senior dogs: Middle-aged and senior dogs seem to wake up less often during the night and sleep later in the morning.

ZZZzzzz

Surprising facts about dog kisses

It's great if your pooch wants to give you a kiss, and vice versa. But once you start, be careful not to smother them with affection – this can make them feel uncomfortable, and they may lash out.

Kissing can be a sensory behaviour. Sometimes the only reason your dog is kissing you is because you smell strongly of something pleasant (to them!).

If you praised or encouraged your dog when they kissed you as a puppy, they might continue to act that way as a grownup. And if you were the only person in your household who encouraged this behaviour, you'll probably be the one your dog will kiss more often.

Looking for treats?

ZAC

Why is your dog staring at you?

- They love you.
- They are begging for food.
- They need something.
- Something is missing from their daily routine.
- They're trying to figure you out!

WOOF-
TASTIC!

Stop your dog from pulling on their leash

- You could switch from a collar and leash to a harness – do some research and make your own decision.
- Use a shorter leash for more control.
- Don't reward bad behaviour. If your pooch starts tugging, stand still and don't move off again until they have calmed down.

Where happy dogs unite!

Teach your dog how to hug

1. Get down on the floor so that you are at eye level with your pooch. Make sure they are sitting in front of you calmly. If you want, enjoy a moment of loving eye contact.

2. Have your pup's favourite food treat close by. Hanging on to it tightly, bring it behind your head and around your neck. Hold it in the spot where you want them to nuzzle you.

3. Once your cuddly fur baby goes for the treat, allow them to nibble it a little first, then give it to them. Repeat the visual cue of holding the treat by your neck a couple of times, to reinforce your dog's understanding.

4. Now you can start adding a verbal cue to the trick like 'hug', or 'cuddle'. Repeat the same treat-holding action, use your chosen verbal cue and then give them the treat.

Valentine's Day

We celebrate Valentine's Day once a year, but your dog celebrates it every day just by being with the human they love.

Valentine's Day

TOWN

DOGS IN TOWN

Valentine's
Day
DOGS IN
TOWN

DOGS IN
TOWN

Valentine's Day tips

Keep your chocolates away from your dog. Chocolate is a delicious treat for humans, but it is dangerous for your fur baby.

If you're planning a dinner date at your home and want to add romance with candles, be sure to place them on a stable surface and well out of reach of your pup.

Is your pooch trying to eat rose petals? Don't worry – it's safe. Roses are non-toxic for dogs.

Did you know?

A recent online survey found that most people cuddle their dog more than their partner.

All the dogs in town love ...

GROOMING and ZOOMING

Making the world beautiful, one pooch at a time.

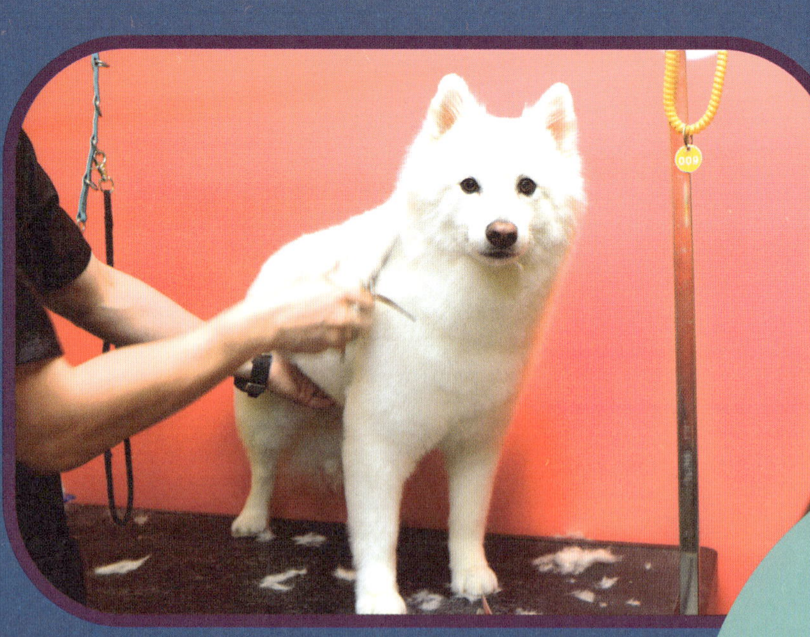

GROOMED TO PAWFECTION

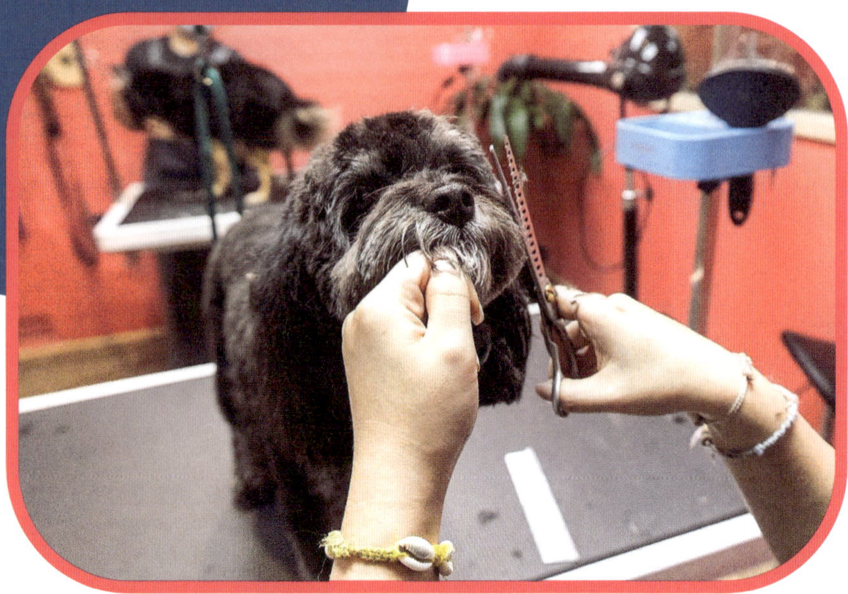

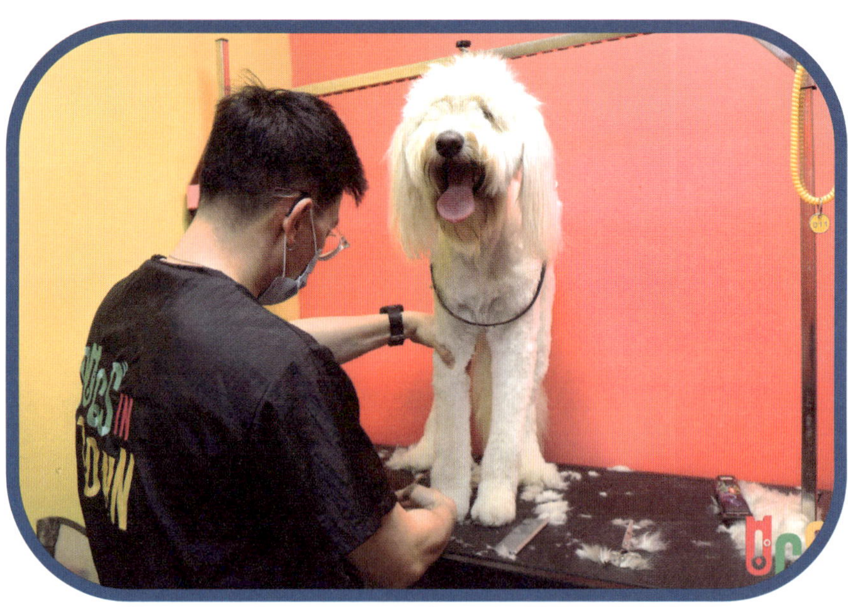

Benefits of dog grooming

- Grooming maintains a healthy coat and skin.
- Matted hair can be dealt with by either brushing or shaving under it, depending on the severity of the matting.
- Grooming will always include a good clean around the eyes and ears.
- Frequent and regular grooming will often be beneficial for any pets suffering from anxiety.

- Making regular grooming part of your doggy's health routine can provide opportunities to detect and avoid ear, eye and skin irritations.

Rub-a-dub time!

Keeping your pup's teeth clean

Brush your pooch's teeth with specially formulated canine toothpaste.

*

Give them dental chews to nibble on.

*

Give them chew toys to gnaw.

*

Send them for regular professional grooming – the groomer will check your dog's teeth as part of the service.

*

Regularly spritz with dog dental spray, which will freshen breath and help remove plaque.

Signs of a healthy, happy pooch

It's common for new pawrents to overthink every small behaviour. These signs are indications that your dog is healthy.

- Fresh breath.
- Shiny, clean coat.
- Consistent lean weight.
- Regular bladder and bowel movements.
- Clean, odour-free ears.
- Your pooch is alert, engaged and interested.

Don't overfeed your dog!

Overweight dogs are more likely to have metabolic disorders, cardiovascular disease, joint issues and a weakened immune system, among other health issues. They are also less mobile, which limits how much they can play, run or take part in other activities.

Did you know?

Dogs' hair grows from about 6.5 mm to approximately 12.5 mm every month. This averages about 4.2 months for a dog to complete their hair growth cycle. However, different breeds can have different growth rates, and other factors like the season of the year, hormones, health, genetics and age affect how quickly your pup's coat grows.

LOVE IS A
FOUR-LEGGED
WORD

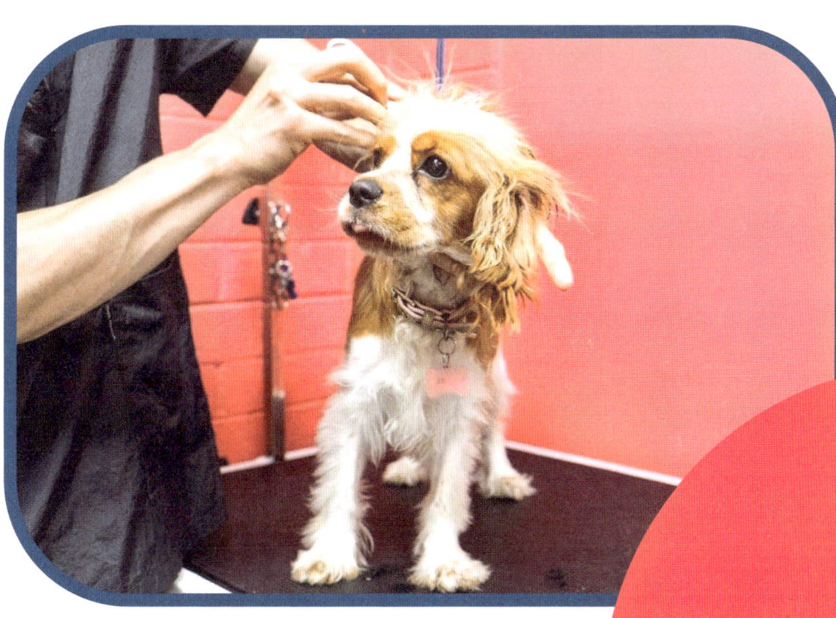

Play for a reason

When petting and having fun with your pooch, especially when they are young, make sure you regularly play with their feet, ears and mouth. By handling their feet, toes and nails, and looking in their ears and mouths while they are having a positive play experience, you will desensitise them to being touched in these areas. This will make things much easier when it's time for the vet's check-up or when they have a grooming and nail-trim session.

I MADE YOU LOOK!

WASH

Wash your doggy's stuff

Germs, dirt and pollen – among other things – collect on your pup's bedding, soft toys and blankets. Make sure to wash them once a week. If your dog has seasonal allergies, this will help reduce their exposure to triggers like pollen.

Stress-less pups

Here are some tips for reducing your dog's stress:

- Stay calm yourself.
- Remove the stress trigger.
- Speak to your dog calmly and offer reassurance.
- Offer a moderate amount of comfort – don't overdo it.
- Teach your own and visiting children to play with your dog in an appropriate way.
- Create a safe zone for your pup (for example, a crate).
- Make sure your pooch gets more exercise, including mental exercise and enrichment.
- Try slow, controlled behaviour training.
- For anxious dogs, consider calming products (for example, in the form of diffusers or collars).
- Consult your vet.
- Talk to an animal behaviour specialist.

Pride

Celebrate Pride Month! Don't be afraid to show your true colours – let them shine!

DOGS TOWN

DOGS TOWN

How to celebrate

- Dress your dog – If your proud pooch is comfortable with being dressed up, one of the best ways to celebrate Mardi Gras is to get them a costume to wear, so they can be part of the festivities. But make sure your pup is happy to wear it. The outfit shouldn't be too long or heavy, so they can still move freely and not overheat. Watch out for buttons, toggles and ornaments, which could all be choking hazards.
- Keep your dog's face uncovered – Although a mask might look cute, it will obstruct your pup's vision. And there's also a risk of injury, as they could get a poke in the eye.
- Dog parade – If you are going to include your pooch in parades, make sure that your dog is well socialised and can handle loud sounds. Bring water for your paw pal, to keep them hydrated. Make sure their collar/harness has your contact details on it, in case your little mate gets lost in the crowd.
- Attend a dog party – We humans like to meet up with our friends at a party to catch some fun, and most dogs would love to do the same! Taking your fur baby to a friend's dog party – or a dog daycare centre that offers a party – will provide them with poodles of fun and stimulating activities.

Pride

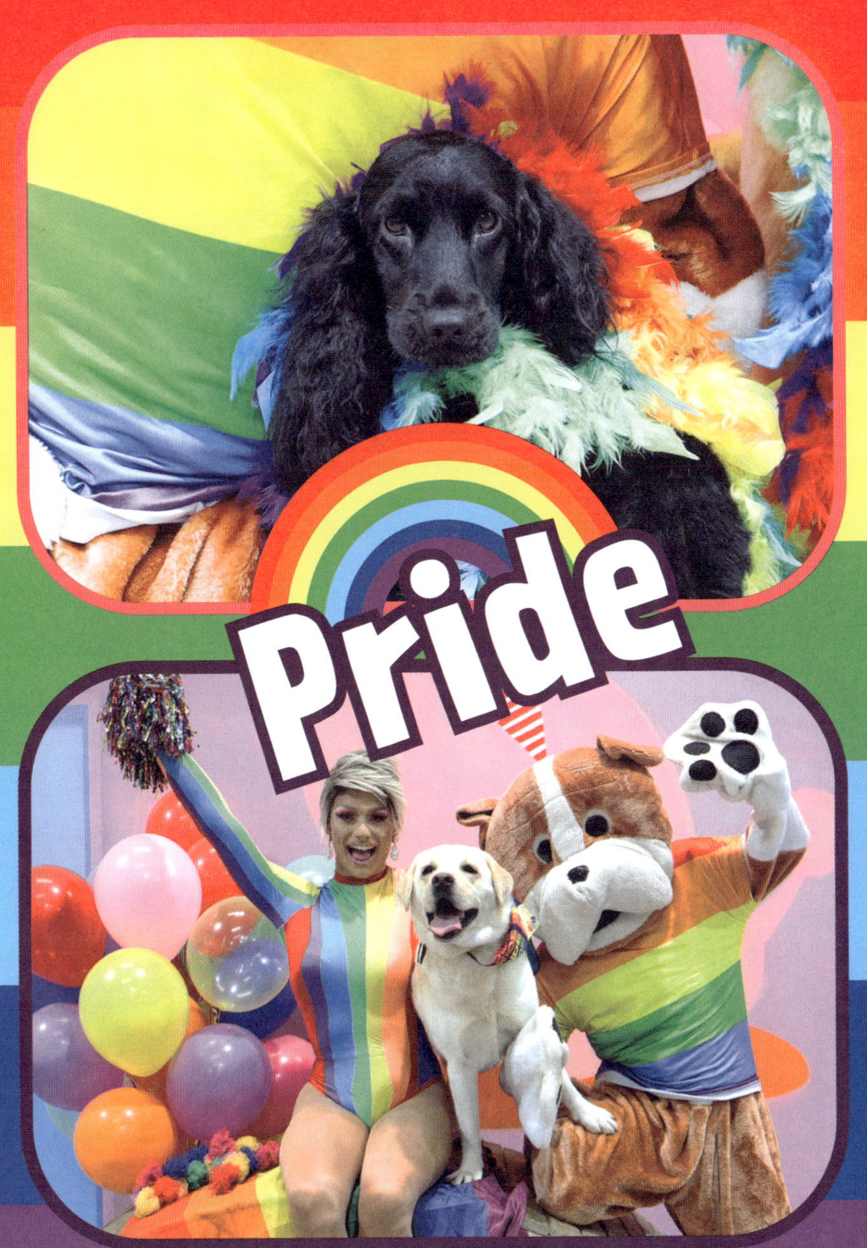

Easter
Who needs an Easter bunny when you have an Easter doggy?
WELCOME

Easter treat safety tips

A warning to pawrents: if you plan to have an Easter egg hunt for your human kids in the backyard, remember that chocolate is toxic for dogs. Keep your pup indoors, away from the Easter eggs, and make sure you count the number of eggs you leave out for your kids to find – you don't want your fur baby to find them instead. For the same reason, keep an eye on little kids while they are enjoying their Easter treats.

Be aware of other things that might harm your dog, like Easter-egg foil wrappers and plastic egg toys – they are a choking hazard for your pooch.

Hot cross buns contain raisins and sultanas, which are extremely harmful to dogs. Keep them out of reach of your best furriend.

Making Easter fun for your dog

Create a special fur baby-friendly Easter treat hunt, so your treasured pooch doesn't feel left out. If you are planning to do this outside, make sure your dog goes hunting before you put out any chocolate treats for your human babies. Put together a mixture of doggy treats, such as chopped-up jerky and dog biscuits, and leave them around the house (or your backyard, if you are very careful) for your pampered pup to track down.

Easter

All the dogs in town love a ...

BIRTHDAY PAWTY

Celebrating our dog's birthday is one of the best experiences we can give to our pawsome pal. Make sure they have the greatest barking pawty ever!

FIESTA!

BOY

DOGS IN TOWN

YAY

Benefits of socialising your adult dog

You get peace of mind

- Knowing that your pooch will behave around children, strangers and other pets is a great feeling.
- There's much less chance of your pup feeling uncomfortable with people and other animals and running away.

You don't have to worry about growing the family

- If your fur baby is socialised, it's much easier to add another dog or any other type of pet to the household.
- More importantly, it's also much easier to add kids to the family!

You create best furriends fur-ever

- If your dog is socialised and you are able to add another pooch to the family, you may create a bond that lasts for both their lives.
- Dogs often need one another for support and comfort, and properly socialised dogs can depend on each other.

Your paw-fect pooch gets to pawty

- You can invite as many dogs as you want to pawty with your doggy or you can attend another dog's pawty.
- As long as they feel like it, your pup can happily take part in the action.

HAVING A FURRY GOOD TIME

salt
PAWTY PUP!

HOBBS
2

PUPPIA

BOY

Basic tricks your dog should know

SIT

STAY

JUMP

DOWN

COME

SHAKE HANDS

NO/LEAVE IT

Quality pooch time

Make sure you set aside some time and create a routine just for your dog, so they get plenty of stimuli to keep their mind and body in good shape. They will always adore you that little bit more if you take them on a surprise walk or give them some playing time. At the end of the day, affection is the language that all pets speak.

HAPPY BIRTHDAY

FIESTA

HAPPY BirthDAY!
Happy Birthday!

FUN
IN THE
SU
WASABI
1

WELCOME
ABOARD

BIRTHDAY

Six suprising ways that dogs show affection

Nosing: Dogs can use nose-nudging to signal that they want your attention.

Eye contact: If they regularly make eye contact with you, they are showing a high level of attachment.

Sighing: Sighs and low groans are examples of quiet vocalisations that dogs use to show their happiness.

Leaning: They are demonstrating their full trust in you.

Rolling: The rollover shows a high degree of trust and relaxation.

Licking: When your dog licks you, they may be letting you know that they respect your authority (and that they love you!).

Birthday
BIRTHDAY girl

FUR-EVER FRIENDS

MAYO
2

4

BEST-EVER BARKDAY BASH

Is your dog lonely? Here are four signs that your dog needs a best furriend

They seem more needy and clingy

They're seeking attention from you because they feel the lack of it – perhaps while you're at work, or when you've been travelling, or if you can't make as much time for them as before.

They are less playful

Dogs are sensitive to your lack of involvement and participation. This is the reason play and socialisation are essential to their long-term happiness and health.

They're more aggressive and destructive

When your dog is displaying unusual aggression and aggravation, they could be doing this because they feel lonely, anxious or afraid.

They're not eating or drinking as much as before

A decline in appetite is a major health indicator that something is wrong. Always have it checked out by your vet, but if there's no serious illness, dental issue, or other reason for your pooch to be tense and anxious, you can put it down to loneliness.

Spring Pawty

Spring is the season when flowers, puppies and happiness bloom!

Tips for spring

Flowers are blooming and birds are singing – it's spring time! The weather is neither too cold nor too hot, perfect for a walk and play at the park. But the warmer weather should also serve as a reminder of several seasonal issues for our canine friends, such as allergies and ticks! As a pet pawrent, you should prepare your puppy for spring and make sure they are safe while having fun.

Things to do

Keep your dog well groomed. Fur shedding will be more noticeable in the warm weather, as your puppy's body adapts to the higher temperatures. Regular bathing and grooming will help them to feel comfortable.

Protect your pooch from fleas and ticks. These insects are active in spring – and they can make your pet dangerously ill. Exercise caution when you take your pooch outside, and make sure they have been treated with appropriate flea and tick protection, as some bloodsuckers may carry harmful parasites.

Dogs don't get hay fever – but in the spring, when the air is filled with pollen, they can get a very uncomfortable itch and even red, watery eyes.

Spring Pawty

HALLOWEEN
Trick or doggy treat!

HAPPY HALLOWEEN

HAPPY HALLOWEEN

Halloween safety tips

Lollies and toffees can cause serious problems for your pup, who might be attracted by the smell. These sweet treats are a choking hazard if swallowed. They also contain some ingredients that are harmful for dogs – so keep them away from each other. And chocolates are just as dangerous.

Your dog may look cute in a Halloween outfit, but if they are not comfortable wearing it, don't make them put it on.

If you plan to attend a furry Halloween pawty, make sure your dog is already well socialised. Seeing humans and their fur babies dressed up in spooky outfits and masks can be scary and stressful for your pooch, as well as for you!

Your pup might be disturbed by the front door bell ringing every few minutes, so make sure they have a quiet place to relax in and give them lots of love.

HALLOWEEN

All the dogs in town love ...

OUTDOOR ADVENTURES

Tongues-out time! For active dogs who love to swim, hike, play and explore, dynamic doggy field trips are a chance to unleash fun!

Dirty paws mean
happy doggies

What NOT to do when you are walking your doggy!

USING A SHORT LEASH Leashes under 1 metre in length are fine for walking your pup on a busy city street, but if you want your dog to enjoy a stroll somewhere quieter, give them more scope to wander.

SAYING 'NO' TO SNIFFING Scent plays a major part in how our dogs sense the world around them. And sniffing is also a simple way for your pooch's brain to get a workout.

USING OUTDATED EQUIPMENT In the past, painful choke collars were seen as the only option for a dog that pulled on their leash. Fortunately, anti-pull technology has come a long way since then!

ZONING OUT DURING YOUR WALK Prevent your paw pal from picking up harmful items, such as chicken bones and pieces of plastic, by staying focused on your pooch when you are out on walks.

TALKING ON THE PHONE Your walks are an important bonding time with your best furriend. Save the chat for later!

NO BORING MOMENTS

TOWN

Activities for pooches

Play catch and fetch This is also a good cardio exercise for your pup.

★

Tug of war This activity boosts your paw pal's confidence and strengthens the bond between you and them.

★

Water play Introduce your dog to water play, and let them know that water is fun and exciting. Taking them swimming is one of the most complete exercises for them.

★

Bubble catch Bubble catch is a great outdoor activity for your furriend, as it encourages brain and body coordination. Just be mindful of the product you use: be sure it's a non-toxic brand that is specially formulated for dogs.

★

Sand pit It's natural for your pooch to dig. Building a safe sand pit is a great way to redirect your dog's digging energy!

Teach your doggy how to jump

YOU WILL NEED:
A dog. A touch stick (also called a target stick). A clicker.

1. Hold your touch stick in the air, high enough that your pup has to jump to touch it. As soon as their legs leave the ground, click and give your pooch a treat. If they're having difficulty, hold your touch stick closer to the ground. Then gradually raise it to make your dog jump higher.

2. Continue this activity, while also giving your dog a verbal command to jump. Gradually stop using the touch stick and use your command instead. Click and give them a treat whenever they jump.

DOGS IN TOWN
DOGS IN TOWN

TOWN

TONGUES OUT!

DOGS IN TOWN

DOGS IN TOWN

Doggy first-aid kit

You might already have your own first-aid kit, but consider what you might need for your pooch as well. Just by throwing in a few things, you can make a dog-friendly first-aid kit that will allow you to treat some minor cuts and ailments. These items include: tweezers, cotton wool, gauze bandages, adhesive tape, sterile saline solution to flush out wounds/eyes/mouth, protective rubber gloves (to keep your hands clean) and blunt-ended scissors.

UNLEASH FUN!

DOGS IN
TOW

Keep them hydrated

A general rule of thumb is that a dog needs 70 ml of water per kilogram of body weight, so a 4.5 kg dog needs two bowls a day, and a 35 kg dog needs ten!

FITNESS
DOGS

Teach your pup to play catch

1. Stand a short distance away from your furriend, holding a tasty treat. Throw the treat to them. If they don't catch it, take the treat away and try again. If they do catch it, praise them and give them another treat!

2. Keep at it until your paw pal is regularly catching the treats. Start saying 'Catch' while performing this activity.

3. Now give your dog the command 'Catch' and then throw the treat. Show them lots of appreciation if they catch the treat on your command.

4. You can start using other objects like tennis balls and dog toys to give your pup more experience with catching different objects. The more often your clever companion plays catch, the better they will get.

Christmas
Santa Paws is coming to Dogs in Town!

Christmas

'tis the season to be jolly, paw lalalala-lalalala!

Holiday season tips

- If you have Christmas lights on your Christmas tree, avoid an accident by making sure you never leave your pooch alone with the tree.
- Hosting a party at your house can make your fur baby feel anxious. Here are some things to prevent this:
  - Instruct your guests not to feed any of your human party food to your dog.
  - Make sure your furriend has a private space to retreat to.
  - Avoid playing music too loudly.
  - Give your pup some chew treats and toys to keep them busy while you party.

MEET SOME OF THE DOGS IN TOWN

It's time to introduce a few of the pawsome pups who let us join their pawty!

Floyd
Rhodesian Ridgeback

Harvey
German Shepherd

Eevee
Toy Poodle

Blue Ivy
Border Collie

Dixie
Cavalier King Charles Spaniel

Reggie
Labrador

Monty
Dachshund

Archie
Schnauzer

Rocco
Chihuahua

Sesame
Miniature Australian Shepherd

Willow
German Shorthaired Pointer

Mochi
Shiba Inu

Frankie
Terrier X

Venus
Golden Retriever

Captain
Border Collie

Zena
Italian Greyhound

Lilah
Labrador

Wolfie
Labrador

Baloo
Airedale Terrier

Jack
Border Collie

Ralph
Moodle X Malshi

Indy
Irish Setter

Rafferty
West Highland
White Terrier

Bentley
Beagle

Migo
Pembroke Welsh
Corgi

Chester
Pembroke Welsh
Corgi

Kiwi
French Bulldog

MEET SOME OF THE DOGS IN TOWN

Tofu
French Bulldog

Humphrey
Groodle

Baxter
Boston Terrier

Shiro
Japanese Spitz

Sara Blu
Staffordshire Bull Terrier

Mocha
Cavalier King Charles Spaniel

Louis
Toy Poodle

Lily
Cavoodle

Frida
Whippet

Hanul
Border Collie

Byron
Border Collie

Charlie
Border Collie

Java
Cavalier King Charles Spaniel

Nano
Jack Russell X

Whisky
Cocker Spaniel

Bruno
Beagle

Jada
Beagle

Rosie
Cavoodle

Chuck
Bulldog

Little Josh
Maltese Terrier

Agnes
Cocker Spaniel

Lennon
Labrador X

Ted
Bichon Frise

Stella
Jack Russell Terrier

Honey
Collie

Freda
Cavoodle

Bento
Shiba Inu

Yuki
Pomeranian X Husky

Toffee
Cavalier King Charles Spaniel

Lola
Great Dane

Ani
Border Collie

Tabasco
Corgi

Cruz
Staffordshire Bull Terrier

Billy
Labrador

Cooper
Dachshund

Lewis
Cavoodle

Memphis
Pomeranian

Luna
Border Collie

Leo
Pug X French Bulldog

Charlie
Basenji

Stormi
Cavoodle

Spaghetti
Labradoodle

Lottie
Schnauzer

Shelby
Staffordshire Bull Terrier

George
Spoodle

Bryn
Whippet

Benji
Whippet

Bob
Pomeranian

Benee
Dalmatian

Pepe
Pomeranian

Oscar
Boston Terrier

Poppy
Beagle

Billie
Poochon

Mocha
Cavalier King Charles Spaniel

Baci
Dalmatian

Crabtree
Bordoodle

Chewy
Labrador

Dave
Cocker Spaniel

Lil
Cocker Spaniel

Hector
Staffordshire Bull Terrier

Mabel
American Staffordshire Terrier

Coco
Chesapeake Bay Retriever

Maggie
Wheaten Terrier

Dustie
Shepadoodle

Pickles
Groodle

Ridley
Bulldog

Lola
Miniature Dachshund

Alfie
Siberian Husky

Alpha
Husky

Charlie
Shitzu X

Baxter
Terrier

Charlie
Groodle

Atticus
Spoodle

Jack
Spoodle

Benny
Keeshond

Bobbi
Chow Chow

Wasabi
Cavoodle

Diego
Pembroke Welsh Corgi

Freya
American Staffordshire Terrier

Maggie
Schnauzer

Charlie
Cocker Spaniel

Dusty
Moodle

Buffy
Cavoodle

Stella
French Bulldog

Basil
Schnoodle

Hobbs
Irish Setter X German Shepherd

Minnie
French Bulldog

Lulu
Labradoodle

Jeffrey
Dachsnoodle

Maya
Bulldog

Mayo
Cavoodle

Sage
French Bulldog

Pepper
French Bulldog

Nahuel
Cavoodle

Kora
French Bulldog

Tama
French Bulldog

Miffmoff
Labrador

Scout
Cavoodle

Pugsley
Pug

Wednesday
Pug

Luca
Lagotto

Nelly
Cavoodle

Harvey
Whippet

Suki
Cavoodle

Doug
Cocker Spaniel

Chase
Beaglier

Cashew
Kelpie X

Nala
Labrador X

Archie
Labradoodle

Ziggy
Cavador

Cadillac
Pomeranian

Willa
Labradoodle

Ghost
Samoyed

Dobby
Staffordshire Bull Terrier X

Baxter
British Staffordshire Bull Terrier

Finn
Labradoodle

Hank
Bulldog

Missy
Greyhound

Isaac
Groodle

Tipsy
Kelpie

Rockstar
British Staffordshire Bull Terrier

Monte
Kelpie

Bodhi
Mixed Breed

Tillee
Bulldog

Arabella
Cocker Spaniel X Cavoodle

Iggy
Bull Terrier

Morty
Golden Retriever

Gypsy
Staffordshire Bull Terrier

Nina
Vizsla

Yuki
Bulldog X Boxer X Cattle Dog

Zola
Border Collie

Zac
Bull Arab

Pablo
Husky

Daisy
Beaglier

Adonis
Spoodle

Rose
American Staffordshire Terrier

Puki
Cavalier King Charles Spaniel

Schnookles
Cavalier King Charles Spaniel

WELCOME
ON BOARD

THANK YOU

Building a brand is like bringing a new puppy into your home. You nurture the little ball of fur, smother it with love, and then Mister Floppy Ears pees on your carpet. You clean it up, start again and before you know it, they're sitting, shaking paws and jumping through hoops.

Even though creating Dogs in Town has been a long journey with many 'messes' and successes, we're so grateful to look back and see how far we've come.

From our early days, walking dogs with our first brand, Fitness Dogs, to opening our third Dogs in Town location, we keep looking for more ways to provide the best-quality dog services.

There's no such thing as too many happy dogs and happy families, right? We think so too, which is why we're opening many new facilities across Australia. Imagine all those pristinely groomed doggies wagging their tails and running around the play yard!

We'd like to say a huge thank you to everyone in the Dogs in Town family who have allowed us to show off their beloved pooches playing, pawtying, being pampered, and simply being their best and happiest doggy selves, in this book. And the same goes for all our two-legged friends, team members and supporters who appear in these pages.

Finally, we'd like to say a gigantic thank you to our suppliers, the 6000+ families who trust us with their pawsome pals every day, and our exceptional team who show us time and time again what Dogs in Town is all about.

Thanks for being part of this wooftastic journey – we can't wait for what comes next!

Gus and Jakub

An imprint of Bonnier Books UK
Level 45, World Square,
680 George Street
Sydney NSW 2000
www.echopublishing.com.au

Bonnier Books UK
4th Floor, Victoria House,
Bloomsbury Square
London WC1B 4DA
www.bonnierbooks.co.uk

Echo Publishing acknowledges the traditional custodians of Country throughout Australia. We recognise their continuing connection to land, sea and waters. We pay our respects to Elders past and present.

First published 2023

Printed and bound in China by Toppan Leefung Printing Ltd

Cover and internal page design by transformer.com.au

A catalogue entry for this book is available from the National Library of Australia

ISBN: 9781760688400 (paperback)

 echo_publishing

 echopublishingaustralia

 echopublishing